FUNDS TO PURCHASE
THIS BOOK WERE
PROVIDED BY A
40TH ANNIVERSARY GRANT
FROM THE
FOELLINGER FOUNDATION.

THE UNTAMED WORLD

Great White Sharks

Marie Levine

RSVP

**RAINTREE
STECK-VAUGHN**
PUBLISHERS
The Steck-Vaughn Company

Austin, Texas

Published by Raintree Steck-Vaughn Publishers, an imprint of Steck-Vaughn Company.

Library of Congress Cataloging-in-Publication Data
Levine, Marie.
     Great white sharks / Marie Levine.
        p.   cm. -- (The untamed world)
     Includes bibliographical references (p. 63) and index.
     Summary: Examines the life, environment, habits, and endangered status of the great white shark.
     ISBN 0-8172-4569-3
     1. White shark--Juvenile literature. 2. Endangered species--Juvenile literature. [1. White shark. 2. Sharks. 3. Endangered species.] I. Title. II. Series.
     QL638.95.L3L48   1998
     597.3'3--dc21

                                  97-11463
                                  CIP
                                  AC

Printed and bound in Canada
1234567890 01 00 99 98 97

Project Editor
Lauri Seidlitz

Design and Illustration
Warren Clark

Raintree Steck-Vaughn Publishers Editor
Kathy DeVico

Copy Editors
Janice Parker, Leslie Strudwick

Layout
Chris Bowerman

Consultants
Dr. Leonard J.V. Compagno has written numerous articles and books on sharks, including the *Catalogue of World Sharks*. He is currently Director of the Shark Research Centre in Cape Town, South Africa.

We would like to thank Janice Parker for her work on the initial draft of this volume.

Acknowledgment
The publisher wishes to thank Warren Rylands for inspiring this series.

Photograph Credits

Scot Anderson: pages 14, 22, 35, 40; **Archive Photos**: page 48; **Frank S. Balthis**: pages 37, 52; **Digital Stock Corporation**: pages cover, 6, 7 (right), 7 (left), 10, 19 (right), 19 (left), 25, 29, 32, 43, 51, 56, 59, 60, 61; **International Game Fish Association**: page 53; **Ivy Images**: pages 23, 41 (James D. Watt), 38 (Scot Anderson); **Amos Nachoum Photography**: pages 5, 13, 17, 36; **Carl Roessler**: pages 34, 42, 54; **Tom Stack and Associates**: page 21 (David B. Fleetham); **Visuals Unlimited**: page 8 (A. Kerstitch); **F. Stuart Westmorland**: pages 11, 12, 20, 24, 28, 30.

Every reasonable effort has been made to trace ownership and to obtain permission to reprint copyright material. The publishers would be pleased to have any errors or omissions brought to their attention so that they may be corrected in subsequent printings.

Contents

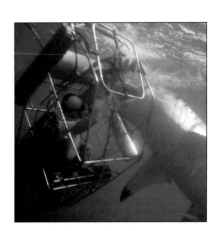

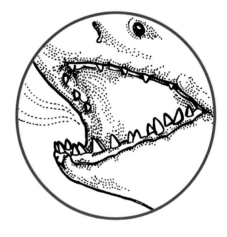

Introduction

People once believed great whites were savage sea monsters.

*Opposite: As large predators, great white sharks play a critical role in keeping the ocean's **ecosystem** balanced.*

The great white shark is one of the most powerful predators in the sea. Of the many kinds of sharks alive today, it is the great white that most often captures our imagination. People dreaded and misunderstood the shark for centuries, believing it to be a savage sea monster with an appetite for human flesh. Today we realize that the great white shark is simply another creature trying to stay alive.

Scientists are studying the great white shark to learn more about its life history and behavior. There are many things we still do not know about the great white shark. How long does it live? How many are left? The answers to these questions will help scientists understand and protect the great white shark.

The great white shark's large size and fierce teeth have made it one of the most feared animals in the ocean.

Features

Skates, rays, chimeras, and all sharks have skeletons made of cartilage.

Opposite: Sharks are more closely related to fish such as the stingray than to fish such as the barracuda.

Great white sharks are fish. There are two classes of fish: bony fish and cartilaginous fish. Bony fish and cartilaginous fish share many of the same features, but each class has characteristics that make it unique. Bony fish, like humans, have skeletons made of hard bones that protect the brain and internal organs and provide support for the body. The skeletons of cartilaginous fish are made of **cartilage**, a lightweight, flexible, elastic material that is also found in human ears and noses. Where the skeleton needs to be rigid, such as in the jaws, skull, and spinal column, the cartilage is hardened with mineral deposits. Skates, rays, chimeras, and all sharks have skeletons made of cartilage.

Stingray

Barracuda and jacks

Ancestors

Four hundred million years ago, an ancient sharklike fish, named *Cladoselache*, swam in Devonian seas. Most sharks as we know them today developed about 64 million years ago during the age of the dinosaurs. For 13.5 million years, from the Middle Miocene to the Late Pliocene Epoch, *Carcharodon megalodon*, the megatooth shark, ruled the seas. The megatooth shark was a relative of the great white shark, and, for a time, they coexisted.

Scientists believe the megatooth shark grew to a length of at least 40 feet (12.2 m). Its teeth were gigantic. Some teeth measured 6.8 inches (17 cm) from base to tip, and almost 6 inches (15 cm) across at their widest point. By comparison, the teeth of a large great white shark are rarely bigger than 2.4 inches (6 cm) from base to tip. The fossilized teeth of *Carcharodon megalodon* lead scientists to believe the extinct shark shared many similarities with the great white sharks of today.

While the tooth of a great white shark may seem very big, it is tiny when compared to the tooth of its extinct relative, the megatooth shark.

Classification

The great white shark is one of more than 370 species, or kinds, of sharks living today. Although all sharks share some similarities, they come in many different shapes and sizes. Some sharks live near the surface of the water. Others live in the depths of the sea. Each kind of shark has its own function in the marine ecosystem. Sharks are divided into eight different groups, or orders, depending on their physical features. The great white shark belongs to the mackerel shark family, in the order Lamniformes.

The great white shark is called many different names around the world, including white shark, white death, white pointer, and man-eater. Scientists use a shark's scientific name to avoid any confusion about which kind of shark they are discussing. The scientific name for the great white shark is *Carcharodon carcharias*. *Carcharodon* is its genus name, and *carcharias* is its species name.

SHARK ORDERS

Order	Families
Hexanchiformes	six- and seven-gilled sharks, frilled sharks, and cowsharks
Squaliformes	dogfish sharks, rough sharks, and bramble sharks
Pristiophoriformes	saw sharks
Squatiniformes	angel sharks
Heterodontiformes	bullhead sharks and horn sharks
Orectolobiformes	wobbegongs, collared carpet sharks, bamboo sharks, blind sharks, zebra sharks, nurse sharks, and whale sharks
Lamniformes	basking sharks, megamouth sharks, goblin sharks, crocodile sharks, sand tiger sharks, thresher sharks, and mackerel sharks
Carcharhiniformes	catsharks, weasel sharks, houndsharks, hammerhead sharks, and requiem sharks

Size

Great white sharks are the largest predatory fish in the sea. Males may reach a length of 18 feet (5.5 m), and females may grow even larger. The largest great white shark ever measured was 22.4 feet (7 m) in length and was estimated to weigh over 4,000 pounds (1,814 kg).

Scientists are still debating which kind of shark is the smallest. A spiny pygmy shark grows to no more than 9.8 inches (25 cm) in length. This is about the same size as a cigar. The pygmy ribbontail catshark also grows to the same size, but it is an adult by the time it is 7 inches (18 cm) long. You could hold several of these full-grown sharks in your hand!

The great white shark is not the biggest shark in the world. The gigantic whale shark is the largest fish in the sea. It can grow to a length of 40 feet (12.3 m) and possibly up to 60 feet (18 m). Unlike great white sharks, whale sharks have a docile nature. They graze on **plankton** *and small fish.*

LIFE SPAN

Scientists determine a shark's age by counting the rings that form on its vertebra, much as you can count the rings on a tree to tell its age. Researchers believe that great white sharks breed when they are 9 to 23 years old. The life span of a great white shark is likely less than 30 years.

Body

The great white shark has a heavy, torpedo-shaped body. Its tail fin is large, crescent-shaped, and very strong. Its body shape is similar to that of other swift-swimming fish, such as tuna. In Australia, the great white shark is called a white pointer because of its cone-shaped snout.

Color

The great white shark is not all white. The shark's back, or dorsal surface, may be dark blue, gray, brown, or black. Its belly, or ventral surface, is white or cream-colored. This coloration is known as countershading. Countershading helps to camouflage the shark in the ocean environment. Looking down into the water, the shark's dark back seems to merge with the dark ocean depths. Looking up from under the shark, its pale belly is difficult to see against the silvery undersurface of the water. When seen from the side, the shark appears uniformly colored and blends in with the watery background.

A great white shark also has black markings on the underside of its pectoral fins. Pectoral fins are used to help the shark maneuver through the water. Each great white shark has different body markings. This helps scientists, and possibly the sharks themselves, tell one great white shark apart from another.

A great white shark, despite its great size and bulk, is a very fast-moving and agile predator.

Special Adaptations

Although sharks are fish, they have many features that make them unique.

Skin

The skin of a bony fish is protected by scales, but a shark's skin is embedded with **dermal denticles**. These are miniature "teeth" made of the same material as the teeth in its jaws. In addition to providing protection, the denticles point toward the tail of the shark and help to streamline its body.

Eyes

A shark's eyes have a special feature that give the fish a great advantage over most of its prey. Behind the retina of each eye are thousands of silvery plates called the tapetum lucidum. The plates reflect light back through the shark's retina, stimulating it twice with each ray of light. This enables the shark to see very well in dim light. Cats and other night hunters also have this special adaptation.

Some kinds of sharks have a third lid on each eye called a nictitating membrane. This eyelid is like a movable shield that covers and protects a shark's eye from injury. A great white shark does not have nictitating membranes. Instead, its eyes roll back in their sockets, which may protect them from being injured by large, struggling prey.

A shark's skin looks very smooth, but when you rub your hand back-to-front along a shark's body, the dermal denticles make it feel very rough. A shark's skin is so rough that it was once used as sandpaper.

Jaws and Teeth

Human jaws are fused to their skulls, but shark jaws are held in place only by ligaments. A shark drops its jaw down and pushes it forward to take a bite. When a shark's mouth is closed, its teeth are slanted back. The teeth become erect and ready for use when its mouth is opened wide. Unlike humans, a shark cannot move its jaws from side to side. A shark can bite, but it cannot chew its food.

Sharks' jaws are lined with rows of teeth that are replaced constantly. New teeth are continually moving to the front of the jaw, where older teeth fall out. It is like having a conveyor belt of teeth—each time a tooth falls out, another one takes its place.

The teeth of small sharks may be replaced every 7 or 8 days, but for larger sharks tooth replacement may take 6 to 12 months. A great white shark may use and lose more than a thousand teeth during its lifetime. Teeth are replaced more slowly as the shark ages.

The triangular teeth of a great white shark may be up to 2.4 inches (6 cm) long. They are edged with serrations much like the cutting edge of a steak knife. A great white shark usually has 26 wide teeth in the front row of its upper jaw, and 24 narrower teeth in each row of its lower jaw. Three rows of the lower jaw and the first row of its upper jaw are erect when biting. This means the great white shark may use up to 98 teeth when it bites.

A great white's teeth are serrated, or notched, so it can carve bite-sized sections from its prey.

More Special Adaptations

Metabolism

Great white sharks are able to retain their own metabolic heat. They can raise the temperature of their muscles, organs, brain, and eyes between 14.4 and 23.7 °F (8° and 13.2°C) higher than the water temperature. As a result, a great white shark is a more active, stronger, faster predator than a cold-bodied shark of the same size. This is because the higher temperatures enable the shark's body to function more efficiently. A great white shark can cruise for long distances at low speeds. One great white shark, tracked by researchers, swam 2 miles per hour (3.2 kph).

Great white sharks can move very fast when pursuing prey. They can even leap out of the water like dolphins.

Liver

A shark can go without eating for a long time because it is able to store nutrients, much like a camel. Unlike many other animals, a shark does not have a layer of fat below its skin. It stores energy, in the form of oil, in its liver. A shark that lives in the open sea, where there is little food, may depend on these nutrient reserves. A female shark may stop feeding late in her pregnancy and rely on energy stored in her liver. The oil in a shark's liver is lighter than water, which helps the shark float. Most bony fish have **swim bladders**. These are gas-filled sacs used to adjust their buoyancy, or their ability to float in the water, so that they do not sink. A shark does not need a swim bladder. Together with its lightweight skeleton, its liver oil helps the shark regulate its buoyancy. The great white shark's liver is enormous and may weigh up to 24 percent of its entire weight.

Gills

Like other fish, a shark must extract oxygen from seawater in order to breathe. As a shark swims, water flows into its mouth, passes over its **gills**, and sends oxygen into its blood. The water then flows out through its gill slits. A few primitive species of sharks have six or seven gill slits, but most sharks have five. Sharks can use their gill slits to control the amount of water flowing over their gills.

Some kinds of sharks have strong muscles that pump water over their gills. Others can rest on the seafloor, where currents flush water across their gills. Most sharks that live in the open sea are known as "ram ventilators." This is because they breathe by forcing or ramming water through their mouths. The great white shark is a "ram ventilator." It will eventually suffocate if it cannot swim forward. It can, however, come to a stop and hover in the water, but it has to begin to swim again soon.

Fins

The fins of a bony fish fold back when not in use. The thick, sculptured fins of a shark, however, are permanently erect, much like the wings and tail of an aircraft. Because the shark's skeleton is made of cartilage and there are muscles at the base of each fin, the fins are movable and flexible. A shark uses its powerful tail fin, called a caudal fin, to move through the water. The dorsal fins on the shark's back and the anal fin and pelvic fins on its underside prevent the shark from rolling over as it swims. The shark's winglike pectoral fins are used for steering, balancing, maneuvering, and slowing down.

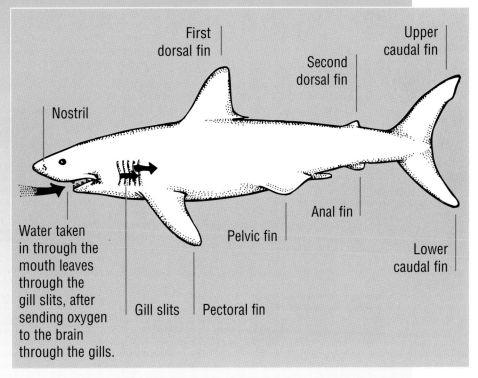

First dorsal fin

Upper caudal fin

Second dorsal fin

Nostril

Anal fin

Lower caudal fin

Water taken in through the mouth leaves through the gill slits, after sending oxygen to the brain through the gills.

Pelvic fin

Gill slits

Pectoral fin

Senses

Although sharks live in a different environment than people, they have the same five senses as humans: sight, touch, hearing, smell, and taste. All sharks, and some other fish, have a sixth sense: an electrical sense. Great white sharks' senses are specially adapted to help them survive in their ocean environment.

Sight

Shark eyes have two kinds of cells to help them see—rods and cones. Cone cells are necessary for color vision, and rod cells permit good eyesight in dim light. The eyes of sharks that hunt mostly at night have many rod cells. Great white sharks often feed near the sea surface during the day, so their eyes contain many cone cells.

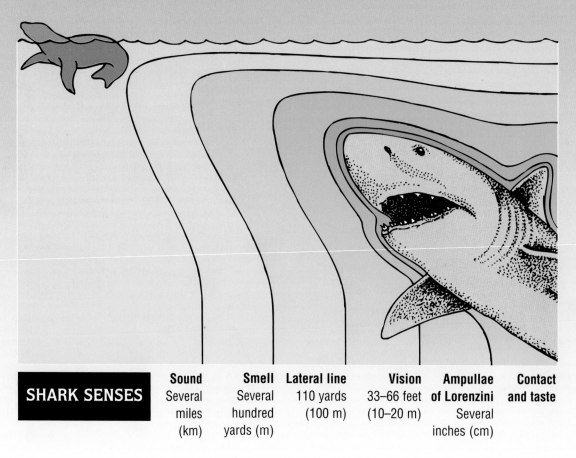

SHARK SENSES	Sound	Smell	Lateral line	Vision	Ampullae of Lorenzini	Contact and taste
	Several miles (km)	Several hundred yards (m)	110 yards (100 m)	33–66 feet (10–20 m)	Several inches (cm)	

When a shark bites, its jaws move forward to grab its prey.

Taste

Like other sharks, a great white shark's mouth and throat are lined with taste buds. A shark's taste buds are similar to those on a human's tongue. In addition, some sharks, and some other types of fish such as catfish, have barbels that function as chemical detectors. Barbels look somewhat like whiskers or a moustache and may be used to taste or smell something before eating it. Great white sharks do not have barbels.

Smell

Sharks were once called "swimming noses" because they have a such a good sense of smell. In fact, at least 18 percent of a great white shark's brain may be used for this sense. A shark has two nostrils on the underside of its snout. The nostrils are nerve-lined folds of skin. They are used only for smelling, not for breathing. As the shark swims, water passes through the nostrils, allowing the shark to smell whatever is in the water nearby. Scientists are not sure how far a shark can smell. The distance may depend upon the strength of the odor and the direction of the current.

Hearing

Sharks do not have external ears like most land animals. Two tiny pores on the top of a shark's head are canal openings that lead to its inner ear and hearing organs.

Some kinds of sharks have small holes on each side of their head. Sometimes people mistake these holes for ears. These holes, known as spiracles, are actually modified gill slits, and have nothing to do with a shark's sense of hearing.

More Senses

Touch

The band of nerves running along each side of a shark's body, from its head to its tail, is known as a **lateral line**. The nerves in this area help the shark to determine the speed, size, and form of an object moving through the water. Sometimes this sense is called "distant touch" because it enables sharks to "feel" another animal from a distance. Pit organs, which are scattered pores over the shark's body, are also touch receptors.

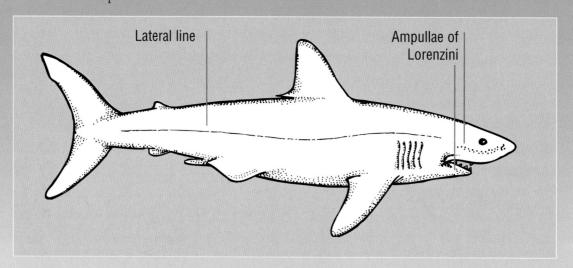

Lateral line

Ampullae of Lorenzini

Electrical sense

The pores on a shark's snout and lower jaw are the openings of the **ampullae of Lorenzini**. These jelly-filled canals contain nerves that are sensitive to weak electrical fields. Sharks use their electrical sense to find food, such as stingrays, hidden beneath the sand. Sharks may be unable to tell the difference between natural electrical signals and those made by human activities. This is why a shark may sometimes bite the metal propeller of a boat. Metal in water also generates a weak electrical field. A shark's electrical sense may also enable it to navigate through the ocean. Sharks, like many other animals, can sense magnetic fields that extend in lines around Earth. These fields are caused by the actions of the planet's core.

Marine Mammal, or Fish?

Marine mammals and fish share many features that help them survive in their environment. The killer whale and the great white shark are both predators that live in the sea. Despite this, there are significant differences between them. Although they look somewhat similar, the killer whale is a mammal and the great white shark is a fish. In the following quiz, decide which statements refer to the killer whale, and which refer to the great white shark.

1. I am a type of dolphin.

2. I have lungs for breathing, so I must go to the surface of the water for air.

3. I have hundreds of teeth, and I am constantly growing new ones.

4. My skin is protected with tiny teeth.

5. I can store nutrients in my enormous liver and use the nutrients as energy when food is scarce.

Great white shark

Killer whale

Answer Key:

1. The killer whale is the largest dolphin species.

2. Killer whales, like all mammals, must breathe oxygen from the air. Great white sharks, like all fish, extract oxygen from water as it passes over their gills.

3. The great white shark has an endless supply of teeth. The killer whale has only 40 to 48 teeth at any one time.

4. The great white shark's skin is embedded with dermal denticles made from the same material as the teeth in its jaws. Although the great white's skin is thin and the denticles are small, they provide protection for the shark. The killer whale's skin is not protected by scales of any kind.

5. The great white shark, like all sharks, has no fat in its body. It stores nutrients in the form of oil in its huge liver. The killer whale stores nutrients in the form of a layer of blubber, or fat, beneath its skin.

Social Activities

Great white sharks are social animals that form complex social relationships.

Great whites use body language to communicate with other sharks. It is a recent discovery that great whites do not spend all of their time alone.

Not long ago scientists thought great white sharks were solitary animals that lived and hunted alone. Scientists are now learning that great white sharks are social animals. They form complex relationships and use body language to communicate.

As many as ten juvenile great white sharks have been caught on a single longline off the shores of New Jersey. A longline is a fishing line with 50 to 100 or more hooks. Groups of eight and ten great white sharks have been caught in gill nets along the South African coast. Marine biologists have even observed great white sharks hunting together off the South African coast.

Body Language

All animals, including sharks, use body language to communicate with other animals of their own species. A shark that is ill at ease may make a threat display to warn another of its ability to inflict harm. Scientists have recorded a number of behaviors designed to establish or reinforce hierarchy among great white sharks. For example, when a great white shark carries prey in its mouth and swims in an exaggerated manner, it appears to be warning other great white sharks to stay away. In another warning behavior, called hunching, the shark arches its back and drops its pectoral fins so that the dark patch on either side becomes visible. Experienced scuba divers know that when any shark lowers its pectoral fins, it is a signal to leave the water.

At Dyer Island, South Africa, great white sharks often lift their heads above the water surface to look at sea lions resting on the rocky shore. Gaping is when a great white shark swims open-mouthed, with its head above the surface and its upper jaw protruding to display its teeth.

Gaping is sometimes seen after a shark's intended prey has escaped. Shark scientists think that gaping may relieve a great white's feelings of frustration. It may also be a way for the shark to assert itself without making bodily contact with humans or other sharks.

A male great white uses one of his two claspers to deposit sperm inside a female's body.

Mating

It is easy to distinguish a male shark from a female shark by looking at their undersides. A male shark has a pair of **claspers** beside its pelvic fins. The claspers are organs that deposit sperm inside a female's body and fertilize her eggs. A human mother has a single **uterus**, but a female shark has two uteri, where the shark **embryos** develop safe from harm until they are born.

During courtship, a male shark swims beside a female. He then tries to encourage her to mate by biting her back, belly, or pectoral fins. Sometimes a female shark may be mutilated by the male's bites. In a few species of sharks, such as the great white, severe bites could produce fatal injuries. Scientists think that courtship biting is therefore rare in these species.

Mating has rarely been observed in any species of wild sharks. The mating of two great white sharks was seen only once. It occurred off southern New Zealand in 1991. At first, the sharks appeared to be fighting. Then, during mating, they rested together, belly-to-belly, for about 40 minutes.

Shark Pups

Sharks are capable of taking care of themselves by the time they are born.

Opposite: Scientists and divers are very limited in how much they can see of shark behavior. No one has been lucky enough to witness a great white giving birth.

Sharks have a low birthrate. Despite this, sharks have survived for millions of years. This is because each newborn shark has a good chance of surviving to adulthood. Most bony fish release huge numbers of eggs into the sea. Most of the eggs and young fish are eaten by larger fish. Only a few reach adulthood. By contrast, sharks are protected during their development. They are also capable of taking care of themselves right after birth.

No one has ever seen a great white shark give birth in the wild. Fewer than a dozen pregnant great white sharks have ever been examined by scientists. From these examples, scientists have learned how, when, and where the sharks give birth. Litters of 7 to 10 pups, and possibly as many as 14, are born in the spring and summer. Great whites give birth in shallow coastal and **pelagic** waters of cool temperate seas. Scientists still do not know how many litters a female white shark may have during her lifetime.

Bony fish that release eggs into the sea, such as these far-line snapper, often live in large schools. Fish such as sharks more commonly live alone or in small groups.

Birth

Some small bottom-dwelling or shallow-water sharks lay eggs. Shark eggs are leathery and have tendrils at the ends so that they can attach to rocks, coral, or algae. The horn shark's eggs are shaped like corkscrews.

Most sharks are born alive. Thin-walled shark eggs hatch inside their mother's uteri. Each pup feeds on its own yolk, which is stored in a baglike yolk sac attached to its abdomen by a yolk stalk. An unborn shark grows and develops inside its mother's body. In hammerhead and requiem sharks, the yolk sac and the yolk stalk form an umbilical cord and placenta that attach each unborn shark to the wall of one of its mother's uteri. Food for the unborn shark passes through the cord from its mother's bloodstream. Waste is also removed through this cord. In some sharks, the cord has leaflike appendages that absorb a nourishing substance called uterine milk.

In other species, no umbilical cord or placenta are formed. The yolk sac and stalk shrink and are lost. In the case of sand tiger sharks, the largest unborn shark in each uterus eats its small brothers and sisters. A mother sand tiger shark gives birth to only two sharks, one from each uterus. In crocodile sharks, thresher sharks, and great white sharks, the unborn sharks are nourished by milk capsules, which are unfertilized eggs. The mother produces milk capsules until her pups are ready to be born.

Yolk sac scar

A newborn shark has a yolk sac scar in the center of its throat that is much like a human belly button.

Development

Great white shark pups are between 47 and 59 inches (120 and 150 cm) long at birth, and may weigh as much as 50 pounds (23 kg).

As soon as great whites are born, they swim away from their mother. Large sharks eat smaller sharks, but a mother shark will not eat for a while after giving birth. This means that the pups are safe from her jaws. The newborn pups are able to take care of themselves. They are guided by **instinct**, but a great white shark also learns by exploring its environment.

Male great white sharks are able to breed when they are about 12 feet (3.6 m) long, but females mature when they reach a length of 14 to 16 feet (4.5 to 5 m). Great white sharks grow slowly, mature late, and produce few young. They are not long-lived compared to smaller sharks, such as soupfin and spiny dogfish, or large mammals such as elephants and whales, which may live over 40 years.

At birth a great white shark's fins are more rounded than those of its parents.

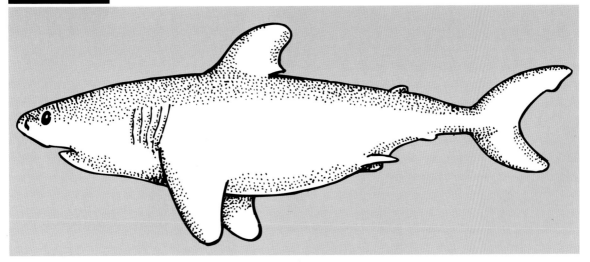

PUP SIZE

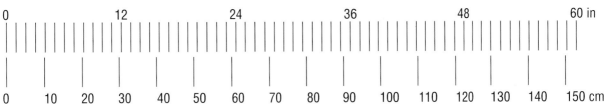

Habitat

Great white sharks live along the coasts of all continents, except Antarctica.

Opposite: Along the western coast of North America, great white sharks are found from the Gulf of Alaska to the Gulf of California. On the eastern coast they range from Newfoundland, Canada, to Florida, the Bahamas, and the northern Gulf of Mexico.

A few kinds of sharks inhabit the deep zones of the sea, but most sharks prefer the sunlit surface waters of the ocean. One kind of shark, the bull shark, can even live in freshwater rivers and lakes. Great white sharks live along the coasts of all continents except Antarctica. They have also been found off oceanic islands, including Hawaii. Great white sharks are usually found close to the surface and in coastal waters. They sometimes go into the open ocean far from land. One great white shark was found at a depth of 4,200 feet (1,280 m).

Most sharks live near the surface because most of their prey live near the surface.

Studying Great White Sharks in Their Natural Habitat

The best way to learn more about great white sharks is by studying them in their natural habitat. However, this is difficult to accomplish. The oceans are very large, and great white sharks are very rare.

Today technology permits scientists to probe the sea's mysteries. Scuba equipment allows visits to the underwater world of the sharks. Scientists are able to study sharks' behavior by using underwater video cameras mounted in remote operated vehicles (ROVs). Sharks' travels through the sea are monitored with passive tags, radio transmitters, and satellite tags. Passive tags do not give off signals. When a shark is tagged with a passive tag, the shark must be seen or caught again and the tag number recorded. When a shark tagged with a passive tag is seen or caught again, scientists can tell how much it has grown and how far it has traveled. When acoustic tags are used, a ship with receiving equipment must remain within 1.2 miles (1.9 km) of the shark. Satellite tags are expensive, but very efficient. They actively send information to satellites orbiting Earth. This data is then relayed to researchers.

The easiest way for scientists to find great white sharks is to lure them into their vicinity with bait, but then scientists are only working with hungry sharks. When hungry great white sharks are around, the scientists in the water usually stay inside a protective shark cage. This cage restricts their ability to study the sharks.

Marine Experts Talk About Great White Sharks

Jean-Michel Cousteau & Mose Richards

"It is our belief that even if great white sharks are not endangered today, they will be ultimately if present trends continue in their exploitation and accidental capture. The loss of such a creature could alter the life of the sea in ways we cannot even imagine."

Jean-Michel Cousteau and Mose Richards are divers and marine biologists who are trying to educate people about animals living in the sea. They cowrote the book *Cousteau's Great White Shark*.

Richard Ellis

"I suggest that the overwhelmingly evil reputation of [the great white shark] is undeserved. It is far from a friendly house pet, but it is probably just as far from the hysterical stereotype we have been given—of a huge, voracious monster, lying in wait to eat us all."

Richard Ellis is a painter of marine life. He has studied sharks for many years and has written many articles and books on the subject, including *The Book of Sharks*, and *Great White Shark*, which he coauthored with John McCosker.

John E. McCosker

"If you don't have white sharks, you don't have a top-level predator. If you don't have a top-level predator, you have more seals and sea lions, who eat more fish. It's a huge pyramid of life that you mess up very badly when you kill a great white."

John E. McCosker has a Ph.D. in Marine Biology and was Director of the Steinhart Aquarium, in San Francisco. He has written many articles on the great white shark, and he coauthored the book *Great White Shark* with Richard Ellis.

Studying the Great White Shark in Captivity

Because it is so difficult to study sharks in their own environment, some are captured and studied in large seawater tanks. Small sharks and bottom-dwelling sharks can adapt to life in an aquarium. But most tanks do not provide the long swimming distances that large oceanic sharks need to survive.

It is very difficult to capture even small great white sharks. Great whites are far more active than most species of sharks displayed in captivity. The white shark is very fragile because its internal organs are not protected by a rigid skeleton. The stress of capture may cause a fatal imbalance in a shark's blood chemistry. During capture, the shark may be injured by hooks or nets. It may even suffocate if it is restrained. Transporting a large shark from the sea to an aquarium is very difficult. The water in a shipping tank may weigh up to 2 tons (1,814 kg), and the shark must be sedated and constantly monitored. A shark's blood circulation is assisted by side-to-side movements of its tail fin. Someone must continually move the shark's tail so that its blood keeps circulating during the trip.

Even when a shark can be kept alive in an artificial habitat, scientists learn little about its distribution, migration, or behavior in the ocean. On a few occasions, great white sharks have been caught and placed in an aquarium. These sharks rarely survived more than a few days, and none lived longer than 2 weeks.

Unlike great white sharks, small bottom-dwelling sharks, such as these whitetip reef sharks, adapt to life in aquariums.

Viewpoints

Should aquariums continue to capture great white sharks?

Many attempts have been made by aquariums to capture and display great white sharks because few people can see them in their natural habitat. Unlike some other species of sharks, however, great white sharks do not thrive in captivity. The few that survive capture and transportation die within 2 weeks.

PRO

1 In order to protect great white sharks, we must learn more about them. Scientists are not able to learn much about these sharks in the wild.

2 Aquariums should continue trying to keep great white sharks in captivity. Eventually they will learn how to keep them alive.

3 By displaying great white sharks in aquariums, many more people can see the sharks. This may make more people care about saving the sharks in the sea.

CON

1 Great white sharks do not survive in captivity. No captive great white shark has lived more than a few weeks.

2 There are probably few great whites in the wild. They should be left in their natural habitat so they can reproduce.

3 Scientists should develop better methods of studying great white sharks in their own environment. Even if an aquarium is able to keep a great white shark, it will not help scientists learn about the shark's distribution, migration, or behavior in the sea.

Food

Great white sharks are carnivores, which means they only eat meat.

Long ago, people thought of great white sharks as "appetites with fins." They thought that great white sharks were always hungry and would eat anything they could fit between their jaws. Today we know that this is not true. Great white sharks are **carnivores**, which means they only eat meat. Exactly what a great white shark eats depends on its size and what is available. Great white sharks eat only to survive.

Opposite: Scientists and others who want to attract great whites often use chum, a mixture of blood and rotting fish, as bait.

Great white sharks will sometimes bite an unfamiliar object just to find out what it is.

What They Eat

Adult great white sharks eat a wide variety of small to large marine animals. They feed primarily on marine mammals such as seals, sea lions, dolphins, and porpoises. They also eat other sharks, such as mako, blue, sandbar, soupfin, and hammerhead sharks, and large bony fish, including salmon, swordfish, tuna, and ocean sunfish. Large white sharks will also eat marine turtles, seabirds, crabs, and squid, as well as carrion, such as the carcasses of dead whales. Great whites have been known to feed from people's fishing nets. Small great white sharks eat bony fish, other sharks, squid, and small marine mammals such as seal pups.

As a shark grows, its teeth gradually become larger and broader. Some scientists thought this meant that a great white shark's primary prey changed from fish to mammals as it grew in size. However, a small shark can eat marine mammals, and a large shark will also eat fish.

A shark's teeth become erect when it moves in to take a bite.

How They Hunt and Eat

Great white sharks take large, active prey by a short, fast dash and a powerful bite on contact. This disables and often kills the prey immediately. A disabled or dead animal may be eaten quickly or slowly, as the shark chooses. A shark may even take one or two bites from the prey and then leave. If a shark misses an agile seal or sea lion, it may pursue it at high speed through the water and even in the air as the prey leaps to escape the shark.

Lions and other land predators tend to select prey that are weak, old, sick, or injured. This is also true for the great white shark, but it is capable of attacking and killing healthy, fast-moving prey. Like a lion, a great white shark increases its chance of success by attacking unsuspecting prey. A shark will often approach the animal from above, behind, or below. It is not always possible to approach unseen, however, and a shark may suddenly attack alert seals at high speed after cruising slowly near them and within view.

The markings on this elephant seal are bites from a great white shark.

Sometimes a great white shark rams a seal or bird with great force and flings it above the surface of the water. While the animal is disoriented, the shark makes a killing bite and eats it, or ignores it and swims away. Sometimes a shark leaps out of the water and lands jaws first on a surface prey animal.

Despite the shark's reputation as a hunter, it does not always capture its prey. Bite scars on some seals and sea lions tell scientists that they escaped a hungry great white shark. Scars on other animals suggest nonpredatory interactions. Scientists suspect that great white shark encounters with otters and penguins are usually nonpredatory. The sharks often grab them, but they do not often eat them.

Feeding Frenzies

When a lot of food is suddenly available to a group of hungry sharks, such as when people dump garbage into the water, some species, particularly highly social requiem sharks, may become very excited and crowd around to eat. The action can become very hectic when there are a lot of sharks competing for food. Sensory information—sound, sight, touch, and electrical sense—can build up and overwhelm the sharks' normal inhibitions. The result is a feeding frenzy, during which the animals can seriously injure one another. Sharks are not the only animals to have feeding frenzies. Many kinds of fish, certain seals, and birds such as seagulls also engage in this behavior.

Great white sharks rarely, if ever, have a feeding frenzy. They are usually alone or in relatively small groups. They seem to have a strong social awareness of one another. This means they either feed together without combat, or they sort themselves out to allow the dominant sharks to feed first.

Although several great white sharks may be drawn to the smell of blood, they rarely have a feeding frenzy.

The Ocean Food Chain

Each living thing belongs to a food chain. A food chain diagram shows the direction that energy, or food, is passed from one living thing to another. The arrows show the direction in which the energy moves. Every animal survives by eating other living things in its food chain. For example, plankton are eaten by small fish, which are then eaten by larger fish. Great white sharks are called apex predators, which means that no other animal hunts them. Even apex predators are selective. They often hunt young, old, sick, or injured animals that are easier to catch than mature, healthy animals. Great white sharks can and do eat healthy animals, but because there are so few sharks compared to their prey, the prey is not depleted.

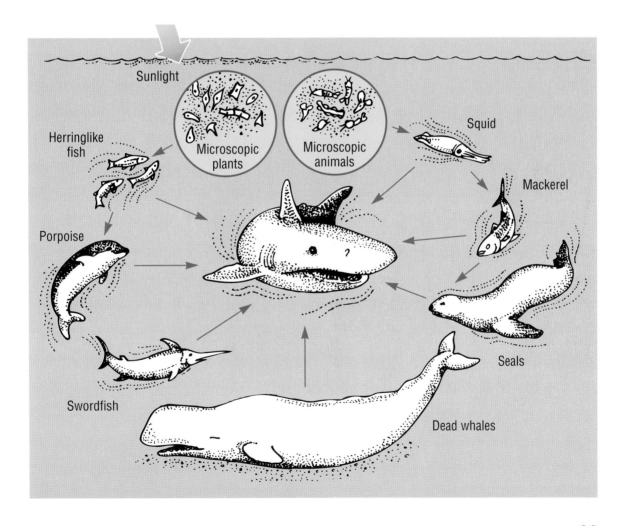

Sunlight

Herringlike fish

Microscopic plants

Microscopic animals

Squid

Mackerel

Porpoise

Swordfish

Dead whales

Seals

Competition

Great white sharks will not fight with one another for food.

Opposite: Although sharks and humans sometimes use the same coastal areas, physical encounters are rare.

Although several great white sharks may be in an area, they will not fight with one another for food. Scientists have observed that a great white shark feeding on a whale carcass will give way to a larger great white shark. When there are two great whites and only enough food for one, the sharks may have a tail-slapping contest. The sharks swim past each other, each slapping the surface of the water with their tails, and often directing the spray toward the other shark. The winner is the shark that delivers the most tail slaps. That shark gets the meal. This ritual combat allows the sharks to settle their dispute without getting seriously injured.

A white shark often has cuts and scars on its head and flanks that are inflicted by encounters with prey or other white sharks. This suggests that when great whites fight, they limit the type of injuries to one another to relatively shallow cuts and slashes.

Parasites and Partners

A lot of what scientists know about things that harm or kill sharks has been learned from captive sharks. Captive sharks have died of blood poisoning, while others have had meningitis, liver disease, and tumors. Bacterial infections and **parasites** such as roundworms have also infected sharks in aquariums. By studying sharks in the ocean, scientists have discovered that the bald patches on the skin of some sharks are caused by infections. Leeches, flatworms, and fish lice may infect great white sharks.

Parasitic **crustaceans** are a favorite food of remoras, a kind of fish often seen swimming with a shark. Remoras dine on leftovers from the shark's meal. The remora's first dorsal fin acts as a suction disk that the fish uses to attach itself to a shark, turtle, ray, or other large marine animal. The shark and the remora have a **commensal** relationship, and may even benefit each other. The remora eats parasites from the shark's skin and gills, and the shark's presence may deter the remora's predators.

Pilot fish are another kind of fish often seen with sharks, although not with great white sharks. Mariners once thought that the little fish led a shark to its food, but this is not true. Pilot fish simply feed on scraps from the shark's meal.

The remora has a flat head with a large suction disk so that it can attach to other ocean animals such as sharks.

Interactions with Humans

Sharks do not compete with humans for food, and humans are not natural prey for sharks. It is very rare for a shark to bite a human, although not impossible. A shark may bite a person because it is very hungry. It is often stated, but not proven, that great white sharks may mistake a surfer or diver for seals or turtles. A shark may bite in defense or as an offensive threat to scare away intruders. Sometimes a shark is suddenly surprised by a diver or swimmer. Like many animals, it may bite if it is scared.

Like humans, a shark learns by exploring its environment. Because a shark does not have hands, it may use its mouth to inspect an unfamiliar object. When that object is a human, it is called a shark attack.

About one hundred people in the world are bitten by sharks each year. Of these, five to ten die. Statistics reveal that you are 1,000 times more likely to drown in the sea than you are to be bitten by a shark. The chance of being killed by airplane parts falling from the sky is one in 10 million. The chance of being killed by a shark is one in 300 million. Most people that have been bitten by great white sharks have survived.

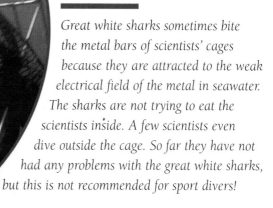

Great white sharks sometimes bite the metal bars of scientists' cages because they are attracted to the weak electrical field of the metal in seawater. The sharks are not trying to eat the scientists inside. A few scientists even dive outside the cage. So far they have not had any problems with the great white sharks, but this is not recommended for sport divers!

Aboriginal bark paintings in Australia sometimes show the shark's liver outlined in the center of the shark. Aboriginal peoples knew the shark's liver contained a lot of oil.

Folklore

People love mysteries, and the sea has plenty of them. Masters of their environment, sharks embody all that is mysterious, wild, and untamable about the sea.

Sharks inhabit all of the world's oceans, so it is not surprising that folktales and myths about sharks exist in many cultures. Even today, great white sharks are the subject of thrilling and very popular movies. These films, like earlier folktales, exploit people's fear of great white sharks.

Although many people fear shark attacks, they have more to fear from being hit by falling airplane parts. One of the best ways to avoid a shark attack is to avoid swimming near animals sharks may prey upon, such as seals and schools of fish.

Island Folklore

Sharks were regarded as powerful beings by Pacific Islanders and were revered or worshiped by many island cultures. In the Trobriand Islands, any teenage boy who single-handedly caught a large shark and presented it to the king was given great honor. In the Kingdom of Tonga, there are legends about Hina, a young woman who became a shark. There are legends of fierce Tongan warriors who turned into sharks, swam to neighboring islands, and then regained their human form to kill their enemies. Polynesian legends tell of the shark-god Kauhuhu, who lived in a huge sea cavern. The son of Fiji's chief god was a great shark named Dekuwaqa, who also lived in a sea cave. Dekuwaqa was also once called Daucina—giver of light. His body would light up to guide Fijian war canoes on nighttime raids. In some of the Solomon Islands, sharks were worshiped as friendly gods, and pigs were sacrificed to them. On other islands, villagers believed that sharks were spirits of their ancestors. Legends on these islands tell of sharks that rescued shipwrecked fishers and children who fell from their parents' canoes. Eating shark flesh is still forbidden in both the Solomon and Fiji Islands.

Long ago, Hawaiians believed in *mano-kanaka*, sharks that could become humans. Even today, villagers on the island of Pa'ama, in Vanuatu, believe that local sorcerers can change themselves into sharks. Shark worship is still practiced on many islands of the Pacific Ocean.

Not all cultures fear the great white. Sea spirits with sharklike heads were carved in the Solomon Islands. Hunters believed such carvings would protect them while at sea.

Myths vs. Facts

Sharks know when a sailor is dying, and they will follow a ship hoping to get a meal.

Ships provide shelter for marine organisms on which sharks feed. Some kinds of sharks even feed on the garbage that humans throw overboard.

Great white sharks will continue to grow up to 40 feet (12.3 m) in length.

Basking sharks live in a similar habitat and are similar in body shape to great white sharks. These plankton-eating giants grow to a length of 40 feet (12.3 m), and have much larger gill slits than great white sharks.

Great white sharks will swallow humans whole.

Although large great white sharks can and do swallow small animals whole, their knife-edged teeth are designed for carving pieces from large prey.

Sharks will eat humans whenever they have the opportunity.

If this were true, shark attacks would be as common as automobile accidents. Sharks rarely choose humans as their prey.

Sharks in Books, Art, and Films

Few sea creatures have fascinated people as much as sharks. Sharks have long been the subject of many books, films, and paintings. In Shakespeare's *Macbeth*, sharks are part of the witches' curse. In Jules Verne's 1870 novel, *Twenty Thousand Leagues Under the Sea*, he describes a large, ferocious shark.

In paintings, sharks are shown as dangers to sailors or swimmers. In Winslow Homer's *The Gulf Stream*, sharks circle a shipwrecked sailing vessel. In John Singleton Copley's painting titled *Watson and the Shark*, several men on a small boat are rescuing a young man from the jaws of a strange-looking shark. The painting was based on an actual shark attack, during which Brook Watson lost his foot to a shark. Watson survived and years later became Lord Mayor of London.

On television, "National Geographic Explorer" and Discovery Channel's "Shark Week" feature documentary films about sharks. The shows are watched by millions of people who want to learn more about many different kinds of sharks, including great white sharks.

Jaws, the best-known book about a great white shark, is fiction and was intended only as entertainment. In the story, a gigantic great white shark attacks tourists at a summer resort. Most of the information about great white sharks in the Jaws *book and films is untrue. Unfortunately, they have caused many people to fear and hate great white sharks.*

Folktales

Throughout the world, people have enjoyed exciting stories about large wild animals. Folktales about sharks are found in many different cultures. In some, the sharks are portrayed as cruel and vicious creatures that should be defeated by humans. In others, sharks are helpful animals that protect humans.

Guardian Sharks

In **"The Guardian of the Islands,"** a great shark named Pursuer-of-Boats agrees to protect the people of Fiji from monsters.

Gittins, Anne. *Tales from the Pacific Islands*. Owings Mills: Stemmer House Publishers, Inc., 1977.

In **"'Ina in Mangoia,"** a young girl, assisted by the King of the Sharks, recovers the treasure that was stolen from her family.

Anderson, Johannes C. *Myths and Legends of the Polynesians*. New York: Dover Publications Inc., 1995.

Cruel Sharks

A young boy outsmarts the hungry sharks that killed his father in **"King of the Restless Sea."**

Thompson, Vivian L. *Hawaiian Legends of Tricksters and Riddlers*. New York: Holiday House, 1969.

In Melanesian mythology, two rival deities created wooden fish and threw them into the sea. One became a shark that fed on fish and humans.

Cotterell, Arthur. *The Macmillan Illustrated Encyclopedia of Myths and Legends*. London: Simon & Schuster Macmillan Company, 1989.

In **"Kaulu,"** a young boy flings the King of the Sharks into the sky, creating the Milky Way.

Colum, Padraic. *Hawaiian Myths of the Earth, Sea and Sky*. New Haven: Holiday House, 1966.

Great White Shark Distribution

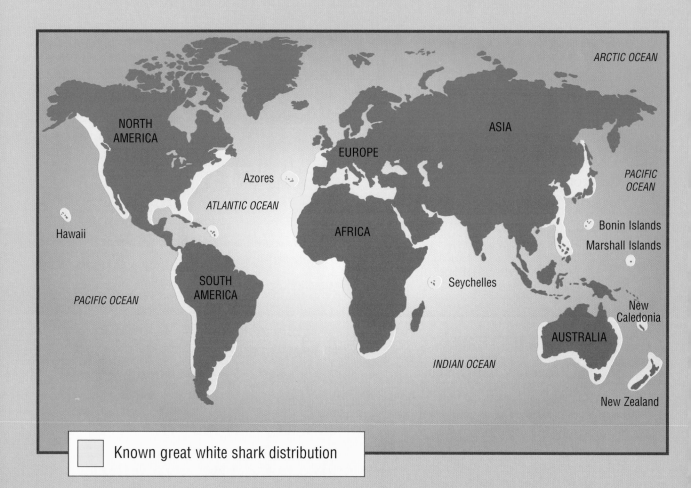

ARCTIC OCEAN

NORTH
AMERICA

ASIA

EUROPE

Azores

PACIFIC
OCEAN

ATLANTIC OCEAN

Hawaii

AFRICA

Bonin Islands

Marshall Islands

SOUTH
AMERICA

Seychelles

PACIFIC OCEAN

New
Caledonia

AUSTRALIA

INDIAN OCEAN

New Zealand

Known great white shark distribution

This map shows the worldwide distribution of great white sharks. Along the eastern coast of the United States, one white shark was caught for every 67 sharks of all species in the 1960s. By the 1980s, one white shark was caught for every 210 sharks, a decline of 68 percent in only 20 years. Australian statistics are even worse. In the 1960s the ratio of white sharks to other species of sharks was one to 22. By the 1980s the ratio was one to 651, a decline of 96.6 percent.

Status

Many scientists believe that if we do not protect the great white shark, it may soon become extinct.

No one knows exactly how many great whites live in the oceans of the world.

Scientists know that the great white plays a critical role in the ocean environment. At an international white shark conference in 1993, the great white shark was designated a **keystone species**.

Scientists also know that the great white shark is very rare. Although the exact number of white sharks in the world is not known, the International Union for the Conservation of Nature (IUCN) believes that the sharks could be threatened with extinction.

In November 1994, the Convention for the International Trade in Endangered Species (CITES) passed a resolution calling for a study on the status of sharks and the effects of the international trade of shark products. A species is in very serious trouble when it is discussed in the CITES forum. Many scientists believe that if people do not protect the great white shark, it may soon become extinct.

Decline in Population

Not very long ago, people thought of the oceans as a limitless resource. They thought there were plenty of animals in the sea, and that they could take as many as they wanted for food or sport. Today we know that overfishing can result in the extinction of an entire species.

The very qualities that made sharks so successful for millions of years now threaten their survival. Most sharks have adapted to positions at the top of the marine food chain. Each female shark produces only enough young to maintain the population under low, natural death rates. Sharks cannot adapt by producing larger numbers of young to replace the large quantities now being killed by humans.

The ocean covers nearly four-fifths of the planet's surface. Its deepest areas are even deeper than the tallest mountains on land. The sea is so vast that scientists have no way of knowing precisely how many great white sharks are left. They do know that there are fewer apex predators than other animals that are lower down on the food chain. This means there were few great white sharks even at the peak of their population numbers.

This great white washed up onshore in the Año Nuevo State Reserve in California. Elephant seals breed in this region and, as a result, it has a high concentration of great white sharks.

Dangers to Great White Sharks

In New South Wales and Queensland, Australia, and KwaZulu-Natal, South Africa, anti-shark gill nets are placed off many popular beaches. Dolphins, sea turtles, and many kinds of sharks, including great whites, are sometimes caught in these nets and suffocated. The nets do not extend from the sea surface to the sea bottom, so sharks can and do swim inside the nets. The nets lessen the likelihood of shark attacks on swimmers by reducing the number of sharks in the area.

Sharks are also hunted for enjoyment. Some people think it is exciting to catch a great white shark and proudly display the shark's jaw or head to prove that they were able to kill it. Until very recently great white sharks were not protected by laws anywhere in the world. Hunters were allowed to kill as many great white sharks as they could catch.

Humans are the greatest danger to great whites. Each year people kill 100 million sharks of all species. Most are killed for food or are caught accidentally by commercial fishers.

This white shark, caught in 1959 in Cedura, Australia, weighed 2,664 pounds (1,199 kg) —the largest fish ever caught on rod and reel.

The Shark Trade

For centuries humans have killed sharks and used different parts of their bodies. At present people are killing sharks much faster than the sharks can reproduce. Some scientists estimate that the rate of depletion may be as high as 2 percent per year for certain species. "If the carnage continues," predicts marine biologist Dr. Samuel Gruber, "species that have lasted some 400 million years could vanish within 50 to 100 years." A few scientists believe that it may be already too late to save great white sharks, and that they will soon become extinct.

Shark Meat

Shark meat is eaten in some cultures. Many people have eaten shark meat without realizing what they were eating. Shark-fin soup is especially popular in Asian countries, where more than 6.6 million pounds (3 million kg) of shark fins are sold each year. Some fishers use the shark's carcass after removing its fins. Others discard it. In a practice known as **finning**, some fishers remove the fins of living sharks and toss the mutilated sharks back into the sea to bleed to death or starve.

Great white shark meat is not recommended for human consumption because it has very high mercury levels.

Shark Oil

The oil from sharks' livers was once used to make Vitamin-A pills. It was also used to light lamps in some places of the world. Shark-liver oil also contains squalene, a chemical used in cosmetics. Today most Vitamin-A pills are made from synthetic products, and electricity is used to light homes. There are no essential products that are made from great white sharks.

Shark Cartilage and Cancer

Sharks' wounds heal quickly, and they rarely get tumors. Some people believe that the reason so few of the sharks caught have cancer is because something in shark cartilage helps prevent cancer. Many sharks are being killed to make shark-cartilage pills. Some cancer patients spend a great deal of money to buy these pills.

Shark Skin

Dermal denticles are so tough and hard that before the invention of sandpaper, shark skin was used to polish wood. Shark skin was also used on the handles of swords so that warriors' hands would not slip when they became sweaty. With the denticles removed, shark skin can be made into a type of leather that is stronger and will last longer than many other kinds of leather. Shoes, purses, belts, and jackets can be made out of shark leather.

Shark Teeth and Jaws

Shark teeth have been used as weapons and tools for many centuries. Larger than the teeth of any other shark, great white shark teeth were especially popular. Some Aboriginal peoples used great white teeth as arrowheads, harpoons, and cutting tools.

Some people believe that wearing great white shark teeth makes them as powerful as sharks. Others believe that shark teeth are charms to protect them from a shark attack. Many tourists continue to purchase the teeth or jaws of sharks as souvenirs. Great white shark jaws and teeth are particularly valuable, and jaws from a large, 16- to 18-foot (4.9- to 5.5-m) long animal may cost U.S. $10,000 or more.

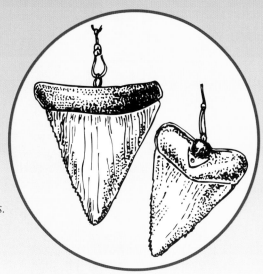

Shark teeth are sometimes used for jewelry. Necklaces of shark teeth are sold in many countries.

Protecting Great White Sharks

In 1991 South Africa became the first country in the world to protect great white sharks. No great white sharks may be killed within 200 nautical miles (370 km) of the coast of that country. (A nautical mile is an international unit of distance in air and sea navigation that is equal to 1.852 kilometers.) Any fisher who tries to harm a great white shark is fined 100,000 rands (U.S. $22,000), and his or her boat is taken away. It is also illegal to buy or sell the meat, jaws, or teeth of a great white shark in South Africa.

In January 1994 California passed a law to conserve great white sharks. Legislation to protect the shark is being considered by several other states. You can help protect all sharks, including great white sharks, by supporting conservation groups working to save them. Refuse to buy products made from a shark. Avoid restaurants that serve shark meat, and tell them why you disapprove. Write to government officials, and ask that sharks be included whenever protection is considered for other marine life.

The great white is considered to be the ultimate trophy by many sport fishers.

Viewpoints

Should it be legal to kill great white sharks?

Marine biologists are concerned about the dwindling numbers of great white sharks. No one knows how many are left, but many conservation organizations believe that they are threatened with extinction. They believe too many are being killed deliberately or getting caught in fishing gear intended to catch other fish. Other people believe the sharks are dangerous to other animals and people. Killing great whites allows other animals to flourish and people to use the oceans more safely.

PRO

1 Great white sharks are potentially dangerous to humans and should be killed whenever they swim near beaches. Protecting human life is more important than protecting the ocean ecosystem.

2 White shark jaws and teeth are valuable. They can be sold as souvenirs. This may help businesses in areas where sharks are common.

3 Great whites are predators that kill many animals that could be used to feed humans. Seals, sea lions, and dolphins are all favorite prey for great whites.

CON

1 The risk of shark attack is very, very small. More people are killed by beestings, or by their own dogs, than by great white sharks. Sharks do not need to be killed to protect humans.

2 It should be illegal to hunt great white sharks for sport because their numbers are decreasing and no one knows how many are left.

3 Scientists consider the great white shark to be a keystone species. This means that the sharks help keep their ecosystem in balance. Scientists know that the extinction of a species critical to an ecosystem may harm all the plants and animals in the entire system.

What You Can Do

Conservation groups try to protect animals at risk of extinction. Some organizations conduct and sponsor research on sharks and also work hard to protect them. Write to one of the organizations listed below to find out more about great white sharks and what you can do to protect them.

Conservation Groups

INTERNATIONAL

International Union for the Conservation of Nature and Natural Resources (IUCN)
World Conservation Union
28 rue Mauverney
CH-1196, Gland
Switzerland

Shark Research Center
South African Museum
P.O. Box 61
Cape Town 8000
South Africa

European Elasmobranch Association
36 Kingfisher Court
Newbury, Berkshire
RG14 5SJ
United Kingdom
(*The European Elasmobranch Association coordinates the activities of all European organizations dedicated to the study or conservation of sharks.*)

Australian Shark Conservation Foundation
P.O. Box 72
Forestville, New South Wales
Australia

UNITED STATES

Center for Shark Research
Mote Marine Laboratory
1600 Ken Thompson Parkway
Sarasota, FL
34236

Shark Research Institute
P.O. Box 40
Princeton, NJ
08540

The Center for Marine Conservation
1725 DeSales St. NW
Washington, D.C.
20036

American Littoral Society
Building 18, Hartshorne Dr.
Sandy Hook
Highlands, NJ
07732
(*The American Littoral Society is a coastal conservation organization. Its members are concerned with the protection of the ocean environment close to shore.*)

Twenty Fascinating Facts

1 The great white shark is the largest predatory fish in the sea. Sperm whales and orcas are larger marine predators, but they are mammals, not fish.

2 Each kind of shark has teeth suited to the type of food that it eats. Sharks that feed on clams have heavy, blunt teeth. Sharks that feed on fish have forklike teeth. The edges of great white shark teeth are serrated, like the blade of a steak knife, so that they can carve pieces from their prey.

3 A great white shark has no bones in its body. Its skeleton is made of cartilage—a lightweight, strong, flexible material that is also found in human noses and ears.

4 Great white sharks form complex social relationships with other great white sharks. The sharks rarely fight with one another, and they use body language to communicate.

5 A great white may use and lose thousands of teeth during its lifetime.

6 Long ago the sharp-edged teeth of great white sharks were used to make weapons and tools. During World War II, shark-liver oil was used in Japan to lubricate airplane engines, and American pilots often painted shark faces on their aircrafts to make them look fierce.

11 Great white sharks, and all other sharks, have a sixth sense that humans lack. They can sense the weak electrical fields that are generated by the muscles of a living creature. Some sharks that hunt prey buried beneath the sand have such an acute electrical sense that they can detect electrical fields that are only 0.0000000 of a volt. To compare, a C-cell flashlight battery produces 1.5 volts.

7 Sharks are intelligent. Intelligence is generally measured by brain size compared to body weight, and by the speed of learning. Sharks' brains are comparable to those of some birds and mammals. They do not rely on instinct alone, but also learn by experience.

8 For thousands of years, historians and explorers have written about sharks and their interactions with humans. Herodotus, a Greek historian, told of sharklike sea monsters that attacked sailors of the Persian fleet in 492 B.C.

9 Many aquariums have tried to capture and display great white sharks, but the captive sharks become disoriented, stop swimming, and die within a few days or weeks.

10 A great white shark is warm-bodied. Its body temperature may be 14.4° to 23.7°F (8° and 13.2°C) higher than the surrounding water, making its eyes, brain, organs, and muscles more efficient than those of a cold-bodied shark.

12 A great white shark can store nutrients in its enormous liver and use these energy reserves when food is scarce. A female shark may stop eating late in her pregnancy, and sharks in the open sea may go for long periods of time between meals.

13 Acoustic tags are used to track the travels of a shark, but a ship equipped with sonic-receiving equipment must remain within 1.2 miles (1.9 km) of the shark.

14 Sharks are sometimes called "swimming computers" because of their highly developed senses. Studies have shown that vision and smell may be particularly important to a great white shark. Eighteen percent of a great white shark's brain may be used for smelling. This is a much greater amount than that of other sharks' brains.

15 Satellite tracking of sharks is extremely expensive, but it holds promise for worldwide tracking in long-term studies of sharks, including great whites.

16 Great white sharks seem to be more plentiful along the coasts of northern California, the Mid-Atlantic Bight of the east coast of the United States, southern Australia, New Zealand, the Mediterranean Sea, and the southeast coast of South Africa. This may be because more divers and scientists come in contact with them in these places.

17 In Europe during the Middle Ages, fossilized shark teeth were thought to be petrified bird or snake tongues, and were used to detect poison in food or drinks. When the tooth was dropped into a drink that contained an acid-based poison, the drink reportedly changed color or began to fizz.

18 European explorers of the sixteenth century believed the oceans were full of hungry sea monsters. This accounted for much of the misinformation about sharks and other sea creatures that persisted for more than 400 years.

19 Marine biologists do not know how many great white sharks remain in the world's oceans, but they do know that their numbers are decreasing very quickly. Humans kill more than 100 million sharks each year.

20 When a VHF radio transmitter tag is used to track sharks, the support boat must remain within 6 miles (9.7 km) of the shark. Radio signals cannot be transmitted through seawater, so the shark can only be detected when it surfaces.

Glossary

ampullae of Lorenzini: Electrical receptors in a shark's snout that enable the shark to sense electrical fields

carnivores: Animals that eat the flesh of other animals

cartilage: The strong, flexible, lightweight material that makes up a shark's skeleton

claspers: Organs along the inner margins of a male shark's pelvic fins. Claspers are used to fertilize the eggs in a female shark's body.

commensal: Two animals that live together without harming each other. One benefits from the relationship.

crustaceans: Hard-shelled aquatic organisms

dermal denticles: Toothlike scales embedded in the skin of a shark

ecosystem: A system formed by the interaction of a community of organisms with their environment

embryos: Unborn animals

finning: Cutting the fins off living sharks and tossing the mutilated animals back into the sea to die

gills: Organs of a fish that allow it to breathe underwater

instinct: A natural pattern of activity or behavior common to a species. Instinct is programmed by nature; it is not learned.

keystone species: An animal whose role is critical for the survival of its environment

lateral line: The band of nerves along the flanks of a shark that enables it to sense movement in the water

parasites: Animals or plants that live on or in a different kind of animal, from which they may receive nourishment

pelagic: The surface waters of the ocean far from land

plankton: Floating and drifting organisms in the sea

swim bladders: Gas-filled organs that enable fish to be neutrally buoyant in the water. This means the fish will not float or sink. In a current, the fish is able to maintain its position in the water without moving its fins.

uterus: The reproductive organ in a female where eggs or embryos develop

Suggested Reading

Banister, Keith. *Sharks and Rays*. Westport: Joshua Morris Publishing, Inc., 1995.

Chovan, Judith L., and Sara E. Crump. *Sharks, Fact and Fantasy*. Los Angeles: Natural History Museum of Los Angeles County, 1990.

Coupe, Sheena, and Robert Coupe. *Sharks*. New York: Facts on File, 1990.

Cousteau, Jean-Michel, and Mose Richards. *Cousteau's Great White Shark*. New York: Harry N. Abrams, 1992.

Ellis, Richard, and John McCosker. *Great White Shark*. New York: HarperCollins, 1991.

Levine, Marie. *Sharks, Questions and Answers*. London: New Holland, 1994.

MacQuitty, Miranda. *Shark*. Toronto: Stoddart, 1992.

Sanford, William R. *The Great White Shark*. Mankato: Crestwood House, 1985.

Steele, Phillip. *Sharks and Other Creatures of the Deep*. New York: Dorling Kindersley, 1991.

Stevens, John D. *Sharks*. New York: Facts on File, 1987.

Wexo, John Bonnett. *Sharks*. Mankato: Creative Education, 1989.

Zoehfeld, Kathleen Weidner. *Great White Shark: Ruler of the Sea*. Norwalk: Soundprints, 1995.

Index